WORDS

An illustrated dictionary for Key Stage 1 of the National Curriculum

WITHDRAWN

0 8 JUN 2022

Consultants: P. Thorburn and S. Cobb

Illustrated by: Marju Rose

Schofield & Sims Ltd Huddersfield

0 7217 0658 4

First Printed 1990
Reprinted 1991 (three times)
Reprinted 1992, 1993, 1994, 1995,
1996, 1998, 1999, 2002

Cover design and illustration by Curve Creative, Bradford
Text designed and typeset by Armitage Typo/Graphics Ltd, Huddersfield
Printed in England by Hawthornes, Nottingham

aA

bB

aeroplane

ambulance

apple

arm

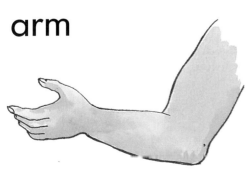

baby

ball

balloon

banana

bB

bath

bird

bear

biscuit

bed

blouse

bee

boat

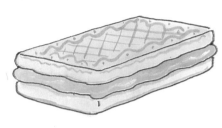

bicycle (bike)

book

boots

brush

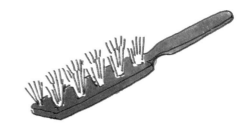

bottle

bucket

boys

bus

bracelet

butter

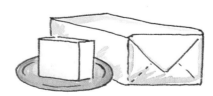

bread

butterfly

cC

caravan

cabbage

carrot

cake

castle

calf

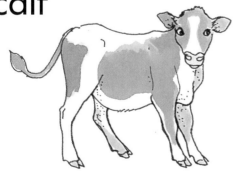

cat

car

caterpillar

cauliflower

children

chair

chips

chapatti

chocolate

cheese

clock

chicken

cloud

cC

coach

crayons

coat

crown

computer

cup

cooker
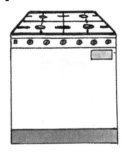

curtains
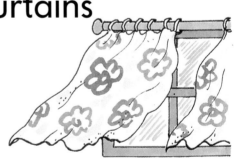

cow

cushion

abcdefghijklmnopqrstuvwxyz

dD

donkey

dentist

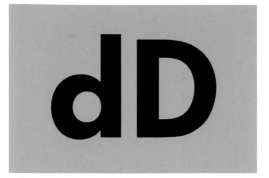

dragon

dinosaur

dress

doctor

drum

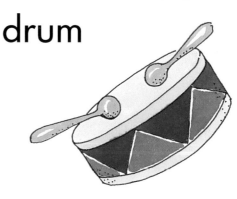

dog

dustbin

eE

eE

elbow

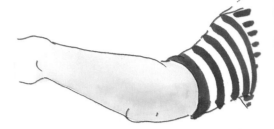

ear

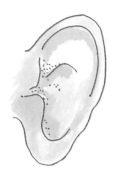

elephant

ear-ring

envelope

Earth

eye

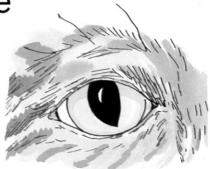

egg

eyebrow

a b c d e f g h i j k l m n o p q r s t u v w x y z

fF

finger

face

fire

farm

fire-engine

farmer

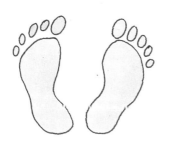

fire-fighter

feet

fire station

fF

fish

food

flag

football

floor

forest

flower

fork

fog

frog

abcdefghijklmnopqrstuvwxyz

gG

giant

garage

giraffe

garden

girls

gate

glass

gerbil

glasses

gG

gloves

gorilla

glue

grape

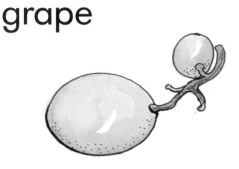

goat

grass

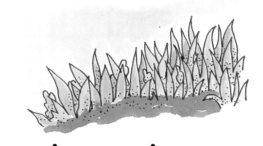

goldfish

guinea-pig

goose

guitar

a b c d e f g h i j k l m n o p q r s t u v w x y z

hH

hand

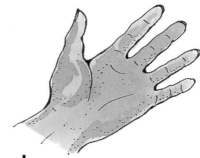

hair

hat

hamburger

head

hammer

hedgehog

hamster

helicopter

helmet

hospital

hen

hot dog

hill

hotel

hook
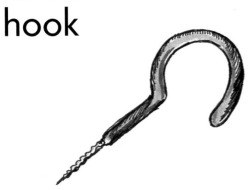

house

horse

hovercraft

il

jJ

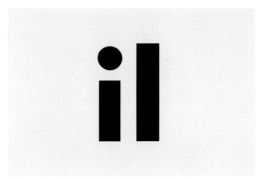

ice-cream

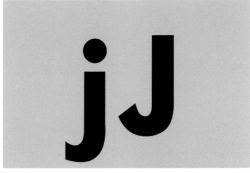

jam

insect

jeans

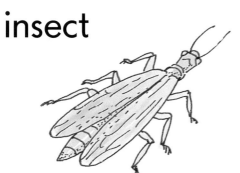

iron

jigsaw

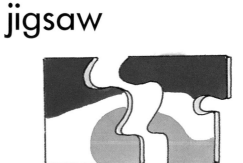

island

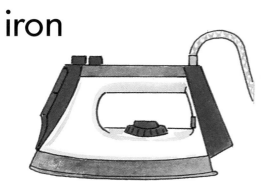

jumper

kK

kK

king

kangaroo

kite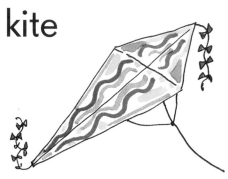

kennel

kitten

kettle

knee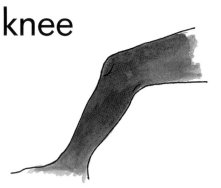

key

knife

IL

leg
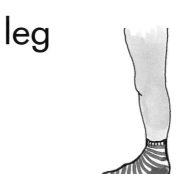

ladder
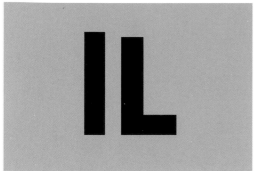

lemon

ladybird

leopard

lamb

letter

TO GRANDMA.

leaf

lightning

lion

mM

loaf

magnet

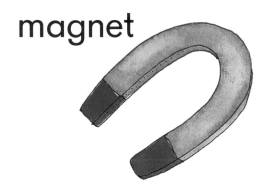

lobster

marbles

lollipop

mask

lorry

match

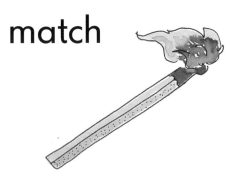

mM

mirror

moon

mittens

moth

money

mountain

monkey

mouse

monster

mouth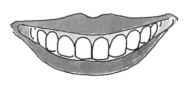

nN

nN

nest

nail

net

neck
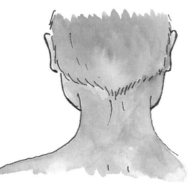

newspaper

necklace

nose

needle
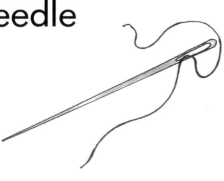

nurse

oar

onion

orange

owl

packet

paint

pan

pancake

panda

path

parachute

paw

parcel

peach

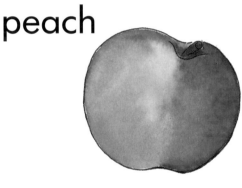

park

pear

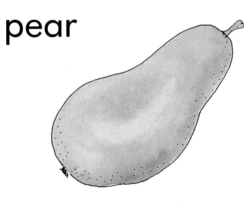

party

peas

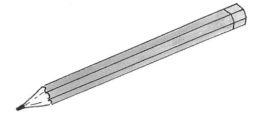

pP

pencil

pig

penguin

pineapple

people

pizza

piano

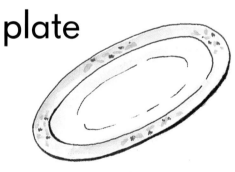

plate

picnic

policeman

policewoman

postman

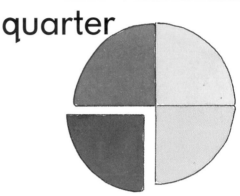

quarter

potato

queen

puppy

queue

purse

quilt

rR

rhinoceros

rabbit

rice

radio

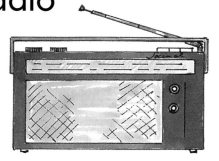

ring

rain

river

rainbow

road

roller boots

roof

sand

rope

sandal

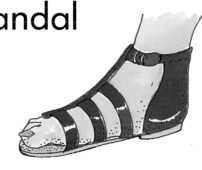

roundabout

sandwich

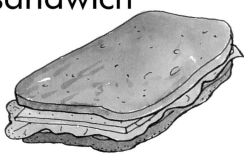

rubbish

sari

saucer

scissors

sausage

scooter

scarecrow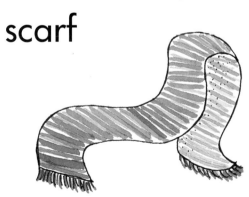

shalwar

scarf

sheep

school

shelf

shirt

skipping-rope

shoes

skirt

shorts

sledge

sink

slide

skateboard

snail

snow

stairs

sock

strawberry

spade
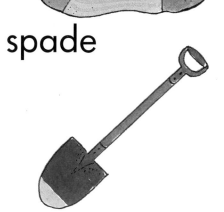

supermarket

spoon

sweat-shirt

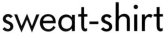

squirrel
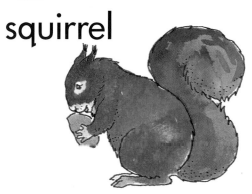

swing

tT

teapot

table

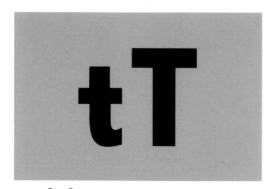

teeth

tadpole

telephone

tail

television

tangerine

tent

tiger

tortoise

tights

towel

tin

toys

toe

train

tomato

tree

tricycle

trolley

umbrella

trousers

uniform

T-shirt

turban

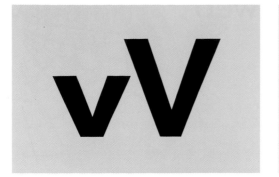

vacuum cleaner

wagon

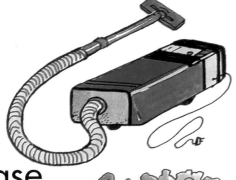

vase

wall

vegetable

wardrobe

vest

washing-machine

xX yY zZ

X-ray

yo-yo

xylophone

zebra

yacht

zip

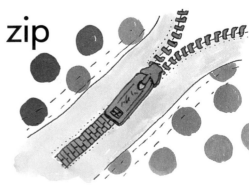

Verbs

biting

crying

blowing

cutting

clapping

digging

cooking

drawing

Verbs

eating

kicking

flying

laughing

hopping

mending

jumping

opening

Verbs

paddling

running

painting

shopping

playing

singing

reading

skipping

Verbs

sleeping

washing

sliding

waving

swimming

working

walking

writing

a b c d e f g h i j k l m n o p q r s t u v w x y z

Adjectives/Colours

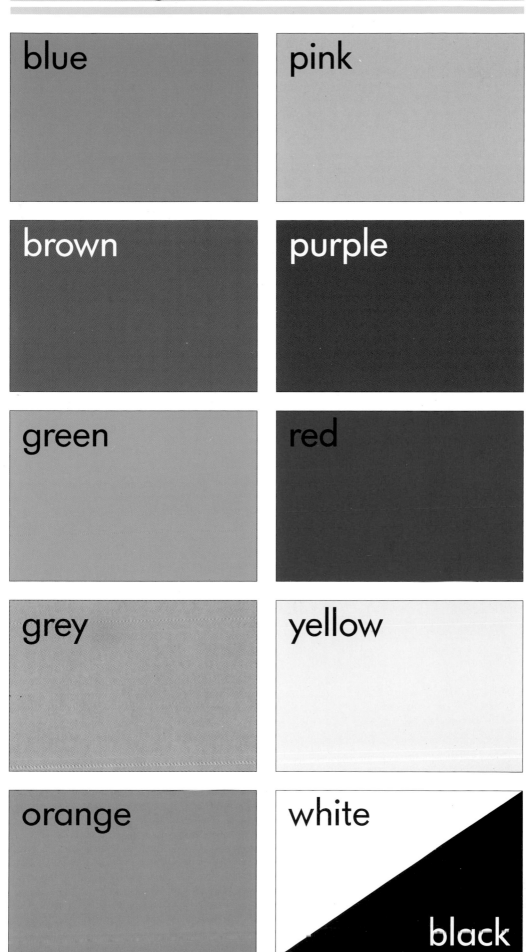

blue

pink

brown

purple

green

red

grey

yellow

orange

white

black

Adjectives

light   heavy

young   old

large   small

sad   happy

cold   hot

Adjectives

fat thin

strong weak

long short

narrow wide

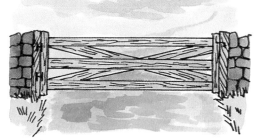

big little

Nouns/Adjectives

one

1

six

6

two

2

seven

7

three

3

eight

8

four

4

nine

9

five

5

ten

10

a b c d e f g h i j k l m n o p q r s t u v w x y z

Word List

aA aeroplane
ambulance
apple
arm

bB baby
ball
balloon
banana
bath
bear
bed
bee
bicycle (bike)
bird
biscuit
blouse
boat
book
boots
bottle
boys
bracelet
bread
brush
bucket
bus
butter
butterfly

cC cabbage
cake
calf
car
caravan
carrot
castle
cat
caterpillar
cauliflower
chair
chapatti
cheese
chicken
children
chips
chocolate
clock
cloud
coach
coat
computer
cooker
cow
crayons

crown
cup
curtains
cushion

dD dentist
dinosaur
doctor
dog
donkey
dragon
dress
drum
dustbin

eE ear
ear-ring
Earth
egg
elbow
elephant
envelope
eye
eyebrow

fF face
farm
farmer
feet
finger
fire
fire-engine
fire-fighter
fire station
fish
flag
floor
flower
fog
food
football
forest
fork
frog

gG garage
garden
gate
gerbil
giant
giraffe
girls
glass
glasses
gloves
glue

goat
goldfish
goose
gorilla
grape
grass
guinea-pig
guitar

hH hair
hamburger
hammer
hamster
hand
hat
head
hedgehog
helicopter
helmet
hen
hill
hook
horse
hospital
hot dog
hotel
house
hovercraft

iI ice-cream
insect
iron
island

jJ jam
jeans
jigsaw
jumper

kK kangaroo
kennel
kettle
key
king
kite
kitten
knee
knife

lL ladder
ladybird
lamb
leaf
leg
lemon
leopard

letter
lightning
lion
loaf
lobster
lollipop
lorry

mM magnet
marbles
mask
match
mirror
mittens
money
monkey
monster
moon
moth
mountain
mouse
mouth

nN nail
neck
necklace
needle
nest
net
newspaper
nose
nurse

oO oar
onion
orange
owl

pP packet
paint
pan
pancake
panda
parachute
parcel
park
party
path
paw
peach
pear
peas
pencil
penguin
people
piano

Word List

picnic
pig
pineapple
pizza
plate
policeman
policewoman
postman
potato
puppy
purse

qQ quarter
queen
queue
quilt

rR rabbit
radio
rain
rainbow
rhinoceros
rice
ring
river
road
roller boots
roof
rope
roundabout
rubbish

sS sand
sandal
sandwich
sari
saucer
sausage
scarecrow
scarf
school
scissors
scooter
shalwar
sheep
shelf
shirt
shoes
shorts
sink
skateboard
skipping
-rope
skirt

sledge
slide
snail
snow
sock
spade
spoon
squirrel
stairs
strawberry
supermarket
sweat-shirt
swing

tT table
tadpole
tail
tangerine
teapot
teeth
telephone
television
tent
tiger
tights
tin
toe
tomato
tortoise
towel
toys
train
tree
tricycle
trolley
trousers
T-shirt
turban

uU umbrella
uniform

vV vacuum
cleaner
vase
vegetable
vest

wW wagon
wall
wardrobe
washing-
machine
wasp

watch
water
waterfall
waves
web
wedding
wellingtons
whale
whistle
windmill
witch
wizard
wolf
woman
wood
wool
worm
wreck
wrist

xX X-ray
xylophone

yY yacht
yo-yo

zZ zebra
zip

Verbs
biting
blowing
clapping
cooking
crying
cutting
digging
drawing
eating
flying
hopping
jumping
kicking
laughing
mending
opening
paddling
painting
playing
reading
running
shopping
singing
skipping

sleeping
sliding
swimming
walking
washing
waving
working
writing

Adjectives
big
black
blue
brown
cold
fat
green
grey
happy
heavy
hot
large
light
little
long
narrow
old
orange
pink
purple
red
sad
short
small
strong
thin
weak
white
wide
yellow
young

Nouns/Adjectives
one
two
three
four
five
six
seven
eight
nine
ten